Meghan,

I am so proud of you and so proud of the young woman you've become.

I love you very much

Mom

June 2002

*I am always here
to encourage you
to understand you
to talk with you
to support you
and to love you forever*

— *Susan Polis Schutz*

For a Special
Teenager

A Collection of Poems
from Blue Mountain Arts

Blue Mountain Press

Boulder, Colorado

Library of Congress Catalog Card Number: 99-34278
ISBN: 0-88396-527-5

ACKNOWLEDGMENTS appear on page 62.

 design on book cover is registered in the U.S. Patent and Trademark Office.

Manufactured in Singapore
First Printing in Hardcover: June 1999

Library of Congress Cataloging-in-Publication Data

For a special teenager : a collection from Blue Mountain Arts.
    p.   cm.
   ISBN 0-88396-527-5 (alk. paper)
    1. Parent and child Poetry. 2. Teenagers–Family relationships Poetry.
3. American poetry–20th century. 4. Young adult poetry, American.
I. Blue Mountain Arts (Firm).
PS595.P37F67 1999
811.008'0352055–dc21   99-34278
                                                       CIP

Blue Mountain Press INC.

P.O. Box 4549, Boulder, Colorado 80306

CONTENTS

7   Laurel Atherton
8   Susan Polis Schutz
11 Char Weisel
12 Judy McKee Howser
15 Valerie J. Higgins
16 Tom Pettepiece
17 Linda Cherry
19 Anna Marie Edwards
20 Deanna Beisser
23 Susan Polis Schutz
24 Bettie Meschler
27 Donna Levine
28 David L. Weatherford
31 Barbara Allene Robinson
32 Sherrie L. Householder

35 Sandra Sturtz Hauss
36 Donna Levine
39 Ann Rudacille
40 Paula R. Hrbacek
43 Pam Lail
44 Rodger Austin
47 Char Weisel
48 Ruthann Tholen
51 Susan Polis Schutz
52 Deanna Beisser
55 Chris Ardis
56 Adrian Rogers
59 Susan Polis Schutz
60 M. Joye
62 Acknowledgments

For a Special Teenager:
a Few Words from the Heart

In your happiest and most exciting
    moments, my heart will celebrate
    and smile beside you.
In your lowest lows, my love will be there
    to keep you warm, to give you strength,
    and to remind you that your sunshine
        is sure to come again.
In your moments of accomplishment, I will
    be filled so full of pride that
    I may have a hard time
    keeping the feeling inside of me.
In your moments of disappointment,
    I will be a shoulder to cry on,
    and a hand to hold, and a love that
    will gently enfold you
    until everything's okay.
In your gray days, I will help you
    search, one by one,
    for the colors of the rainbow.
In your bright and shining hours, I will
    be smiling, too, right along beside you.
In your life, I wish I could give you a very
special gift. It would be this:
When you look in the mirror in the
days ahead, may you smile a hundred
times more than frowning at what you see.
Smile because you know that a loving,
capable, sensible, strong, precious person
    is reflected there.

And when you look at me, may you
    remember how very much I love you . . .
    and how much I'll always care.

— Laurel Atherton

My Child, I Will Always
Do My Best for You

Sometimes it is so hard
to be a parent
We never know for sure
if what we are doing or
how we are acting is right

Sometimes it might seem
like I make a decision
that is not fair
I might not be
looking at the immediate results
but I am thinking
how it will affect you
and what you will learn from it
in the future

Since I consider you
a very smart person
capable of leading your own life
I very rarely
make decisions for you
But when I do
I want you to know that
I have a great amount of
sensitivity to who you are and
the foundation of any suggestions
I give to you
is made with
an enormous love and respect
for you
my child

— Susan Polis Schutz

You Always Have My Love
and Support

Sometimes, it's as difficult
to be a parent
as it is to be a teenager.
There's as much difficulty
in giving discipline
as in receiving it.
Responsibility for
the well-being of someone never ends.

I know that you feel like
you're being held back sometimes.
You are uncertain about the future,
so you throw yourself into today.
It's difficult to be a teenager.
You want freedom;
you make choices,
but don't always want
to accept the consequences.
You look for acceptance,
then try to find ways to be different.
You are afraid to show
your feelings to me,
imagining that it's impossible
for me to understand what you are feeling.
Yet I do know, and I do care;
we'll come through
these difficult times together.

— Char Weisel

Life's Difficult Times Make Us Stronger and Wiser

I see you growing
in wisdom and maturity —
setting priorities,
making difficult decisions —
and I'm proud of you.
I know that
growing up has been
painful sometimes;
there have been losses
and lonely times.
Yet your wonderful spirit
always prevails,
and you emerge better for it.

With all my heart,
I wish I could take away
the bad times for you,
but perhaps it's best
that I can't.
Without those difficult times
you wouldn't be so wise,
or have the wonderful qualities
and strength of character
that make you the person
you are today.

— Judy McKee Howser

Always Know that
I Am Here to Understand

I know you sometimes
can't talk about
what's troubling you,
because you have no words
   that can explain
what you feel inside.
But I understand.

Sometimes, my heart aches for you
and I want to hold on to you,
to take away your pain.
Sometimes watching you
reminds me of myself,
because I have been there, too.

Sometimes you don't
have to say anything,
because I know how you feel.
The closeness that we share
means the world to me.
Please remember that I care,
and I will always be here for you
when you want to talk.
You are special, and I love you.

— Valerie J. Higgins

No matter how old you grow,
you'll always be my child . . .

Though I treasure the way
you have grown to be
your own person,
you'll always be my child . . .

The days we have shared —
growing together —
will continue to fill me with joy.

Through your eyes, I see a world
teeming with possibility and hope.
Through your spirit,
I regain my focus
on what is most important
in life . . .
how we love and give
to one another.

This day, like all others, will pass,
but who we are,
because of the love we share,
will endure forever.

I'll always be so thankful
for you, my child.

— Tom Pettepiece

I Will Always Be Here for You, My Child

You're not a child anymore,
and you no longer need me
to bandage your knees
and wipe away your tears.

Yet I am still your parent,
and just as I adjusted
to your changing height,
I try to remember that
you need me differently now.

We both know that
life has many complexities
that can be much more painful
than skinned knees.

So if you ever want to talk
or just be with someone,
you know my love never changes,
and I'll always be here for you.

— Linda Cherry

I May Not Always Be the Perfect Parent, but I Do Always Love You

I know I'm not always
   the best parent in the world.
I'm still learning,
and I'll never have
   all the right answers.
All I can do is try my best
   to do what I feel is best for you.
And when you think I've done
   something wrong, or I'm not
   giving you the attention you
      deserve, I hope you'll tell me,
because I don't ever want anything
   to come between us.
I love you,
   and I always will.

— Anna Marie Edwards

A Special Thought
from Your Parent

I have often wondered
what kind of parent I am to you,
and if you are learning
all the qualities and values
that are so important in life.
I know in my heart that
I am always trying to show you
how to be loving and caring
    towards others,
but there are times when I feel as if
I am falling short of my expectations.

My wish for you
is that you will grow up
to be independent and self-assured.
Those are two very vital qualities
to have for yourself in order to find
your own happiness.
If you can enjoy yourself
and your own talents,
you will be able to appreciate others
and their special abilities.
As a parent, there are so many dreams
that I want to come true for you.
I want you to live life to the fullest.
And, as time goes by
and you don't need my guidance
and direction as much as before,
I hope you will always remember . . .

I love you.

— Deanna Beisser

I Love You Forever,
My Child

I am so happy
with the direction
that your life
is taking you
All of your decisions and
all of your actions
are so noble and intelligent
I often think about
how you were the same way
when you were little
I hope that you remain so in control
of your life forever
And I want you to know that
sometimes you will make mistakes
and when those times occur
the proudest mother in the world
is always here
to encourage you
to understand you
to talk with you
to support you
and to love you forever

— Susan Polis Schutz

I Want to Share
This Special Thought
with You

Lately, we have had our differences.
You are struggling with this time
between childhood and adulthood,
and I am having a difficult time
accepting the fact that you
are no longer a child.

I know I sometimes say things that hurt you.
I wish I could take them back.
I sometimes get confused
with what I want for you
and your right to choose for yourself.
I forget that the decisions
you make are based on
your own perceptions,
and I make unfair judgments of them
from my perspective.

You deserve the chance
to learn about life, just as I did.
I mistakenly think I can keep you
from future mistakes
and the pain that may lie ahead,
but I really don't know how
the future will be affected
by your actions today.

Sometimes, you may feel that
I can't relate to anything in your life,
but I see myself in you at the same age,
and I want to protect you,
when what I have to do is
find the courage to set you free.
Our relationship is changing,
and so are we.
If we understand each other,
we can see this time through together.
The one thing that will never change
is our love for each other,
and that is all that really matters.

— Bettie Meschler

Growing Up Is Never Easy

Growing up is never easy to do.
Some days you feel happy and carefree,
and other days you feel sad.
Some days you feel confident and
   self-assured,
and other days you feel unsure.
Life can seem upside down,
because you're changing so quickly,
but your life is made up of what
you believe about yourself.

Believe in your ability to succeed,
and you will.
Believe in your ability to meet
every difficult challenge,
and you will.
Believe in your ability to give
and receive love,
and you will.
Believe in yourself.
You are a wonderful, unique person
who is beginning to find out
what the world is about
and searching for your place in it.
Have patience with yourself
and love yourself.
Growing up isn't easy,
but you'll make it.

— Donna Levine

A Message for You
About Learning and
Growing Up

When a child learns that giving
is more rewarding than taking;
when he learns that he
can't control everything,
but that he is master of his own soul;
when he learns to accept
a person whose differences he fears,
and that pleasure is found
in the power of helping others;
when he learns that the value
of one's life is best measured
not by possessions acquired,
but by wisdom shared, hope inspired,
    tears wiped, and hearts touched;
when he learns that happiness
    and lasting contentment
are not to be found
in what a person has,
    but in what he is;

when he learns to withhold
   judgment of people,
knowing that everyone is blessed
   with good and bad qualities;
when he learns that every person
has been given the gift
   of a unique self,
and the purpose of life is to share
the very best of that gift
   with the world . . .
When a child learns these ideals,
he will no longer be a child —
he will be a blessing to those
   who know him,
and a worthy model
for all the world's children.

— David L. Weatherford

Being a teenager can be hard;
that's why I'll always try to be
here for you . . .

My child, you are growing up.
You're in that bittersweet stage
    called adolescence.
New emotions are awakening in you.
Sometimes you feel like an adult;
other times you feel like a child.
There are times of great joy
and times of bitter distress.
But I just hope you know
    that I will always try . . .
to be available for you,
to listen to you,
to be patient and understanding,
to allow you to make your own decisions
    . . . and mistakes.
I will rejoice with you in your successes
    and comfort you in your disappointments,
and I will always respond to you
    in the most loving way I know.

— Barbara Allene Robinson

I Will Always Encourage You
in Your Dreams

I see so much within you:
so much light in your eyes,
so much laughter in your soul.
I want you to have freedom
to experience all of life,
yet I want to hold you close.
I hear the excitement in your voice
when you reach out
    for something important to you
and you achieve it.

I never want you
    to feel unloved,
because I love you more
    than life itself.
I want to wrap my arms around you
so that you'll always feel
    safe, secure, and cherished.

I will always stand beside you;
I'll wipe your tears when you cry,
I'll comfort you when you feel hurt.
I want to encourage you to be
whatever you want.

Whatever you pursue in life,
I'll be there as your friend,
    as well as your parent.
If you ever fail at something,
I'll encourage you
    to get up and try again,
because it doesn't mean
you'll fail at everything;
everyone learns by their mistakes.
I want you to know
I'll always be here for you.

— Sherrie L. Householder

My Wish for You

Take my hand, for it reaches out to you
any time you need it.
Take a moment each day to reflect on
what you have and how fortunate you are.
Take a moment to reflect on what you
want and how capable you are.
Take the time to do things that bring
you pleasure and self-satisfaction.
Take resources available to you and
put them to use for your own enjoyment.
Take the kindness others show you as
a measure of their high regard for you.
Take the insensitivity others may
demonstrate as an indication that
their own self-esteem may need building.
Take comfort in the realization that
although you may not be or have all
you want, you are working at it
the best way you can.
Take pride in your individuality,
your special ways, the beautiful person
you are.
Take my words as loving advice,
because I want only the best for you.
Take my love with you wherever you go.
It has been and always will be yours.

— Sandra Sturtz Hauss

Accept Yourself for
Who You Are . . . a Teenager
with So Much Potential

Accept yourself for who you are.
You are a unique, wonderful person
who is in the process of growing.
Growth can be confusing and painful;
sometimes it may even seem easier
to sit where you are,
instead of taking those
first, unsteady steps forward.
Give yourself time;
making changes is never easy,
and the challenges are difficult.
Learn to love yourself
and forgive yourself;
holding on to guilt and fear
will only keep you unhappy,
and you deserve happiness.

Look into your heart and discover
all the good things about yourself,
because you are truly beautiful.
Don't lose faith in your hopes
and dreams; have more faith,
keep your hopes strong,
and keep your dreams alive.
The troublesome moments will pass;
you will be more open to life,
and you will realize that
you have the courage
to face the rough times,
and make your days brighter
and more fulfilled.

— Donna Levine

Even Parents Can Make Mistakes Sometimes, Too

No one is perfect,
and parents are no exception.
Parents make their share of mistakes,
just like everyone else.
But I have loved you with all my heart,
    and I always will,
and any mistakes I might have made
were not because I didn't care.

I am sorry for the times when
    so much was on my mind that
I became impatient
and denied you consolation
for the answers I failed to find.
I'm sorry for the days when my logic
    was less than you needed.
And most of all, I'm sorry for the
    times when I was too busy to show
you the love that I feel for you —
the love that I can only hope
    showed through
        my imperfections.

— Ann Rudacille

As You Go Through
Your Teenage Years . . .

My dear child,
through the years
I have watched you grow,
each day coming one step closer
to the adult you will one day become.
Now is an awkward time for you;
every teen goes through it.
My saying this to you
won't make it any easier,
but hopefully a little understanding
from both of us will make
the going as smooth as possible.
Being a teenager isn't easy.
I understand that your rebellion,
the fads, and new interests
are your way of becoming mature.
There is a special person inside of you
that only you can find, develop, and be.

Finding that person is confusing.
Much of what you once thought
will be challenged;
much of what you once were will change.
But you are my child,
and I love you.
Nothing can change that —
not your hair, your clothes,
or even when we disagree.
I am so proud of your efforts.
I believe in your ability.
I watch your growth with love and respect.
Having you in my life has made it
so much better.
That is your gift of love to me,
and I thank you, my child,
for that wonderful gift.

— Paula R. Hrbacek

You Make Me Grateful
to Be Your Parent

My child,
you have grown so much.
Sometimes I watch you,
and now and then
I become a little sad at the thought
of your not being little anymore.
But I rejoice, too,
at how mature and responsible
you are now.

As your parent,
I have regrets about the past;
I said and did things
that must have hurt you,
and I often wonder
if I failed you.
But we have many happy
   memories, too,
to last the rest of our lives.
You have given me so much
to live for.
I hope you know that I love you
with all my heart.

— Pam Lail

You Are
My Life's Blessing

I don't know what the future holds for
your life, but whatever that may be, I am
very proud of you. You have given me the
hopes that God will bless you and keep
you in His hands. No matter what you
want to be, you will always be my child, a
blessing that was given me to protect, to
guide, to help along the way. If it had not
been for you, I would not have made it this
far. You were and are a happiness I am
glad to bear. You will someday have
children of your own, and when that day
comes, you will know what it is to want
the most for them, the best for them, to care
for them more than for yourself. When that
day comes, I hope you will fully realize what
a joy you have been to me, and how much
I love you.

Children are God's way to
keep giving to the world to
show how much He cares, to bring a little
happiness to someone. You are the best
child I could have asked for: giving,
loving, caring, sharing, truly my best
friend. I want you to always remember
that I love you with all my heart, and that
whatever may happen, you will always be
the most important thing in my life. May
all your troubles be little, all your
problems be simple; may God always
guide your paths and bless you. I love you,
and I always will.

— Rodger Austin

I Know It's Difficult Being a Teenager, and I Care

Sometimes, I get so caught up
in all the things that go wrong,
that I don't give enough credit
to the things that go right.
I know what a struggle
you are having in your life,
and how much pressure there
is on you as a teenager.

If I could make
your growth to adulthood
any easier, I would.
I want to protect you from the world,
but even if that were possible,
it would prevent you
from learning the skills you need in life.
You are a fine person;
if you make wrong choices sometimes,
remember that they are
a necessary though painful part
of growing up.
Don't settle for less than you can be;
trust your best instincts.
Always make an honest effort
and do your best as you grow up.

— Char Weisel

I'm So Proud of You, My Child

When I held you as a child,
it was like taking up in my arms
all of my hopes for the future.
I loved you so much then
that I felt my heart would break
with the pride and joy I felt.
I wondered then
    who you would become,
        and you haven't
            let me down.
You are a person to be proud of.
You are sensitive, but strong,
with the courage to follow your own path,
to know and do what is right for you.

The love between us needs few words,
but is the foundation for all we give
by being there, by sharing time and effort,
by our talks, and by our caring.
I'm proud when you accomplish things,
but even prouder of the way you live.
Whether you win or lose,
you do it with integrity and humanity,
and I respect that.
From your own efforts, there has grown
a deep goodness in you.
I can wish nothing more
than that your life will hold a future
of happiness.
I love you, and I'm very glad
you are my child.

— Ruthann Tholen

Do your best, my child,
and realize that I love you

Sometimes you
think that you
need to be perfect
that you cannot
make mistakes
At these times
you put so much
pressure on yourself
I wish that you
would realize
that you are
a human being —
like everyone else
capable of
reaching great potential
but not capable of
being perfect
So please
just do your best
and realize that
this is enough
Don't compare yourself
to anyone
Be happy to be
the wonderful
unique, very special
person that you are

— Susan Polis Schutz

For a Teenager
I Love with All My Heart

When I was growing up,
my family didn't say
"I love you" very often.
It was just understood
   between everyone
by the caring and loving things
we did for each other.
But times have changed,
and now it's easier to talk
about our feelings.

I hope it will always be easy
for us to talk about our feelings
and share our emotions.
It is nice to hear the words
"I love you,"
and it is important to say them,
because they are such a special
    part of loving.
So that's why
I want you to know
that I am thinking about you,
I am caring about you,
and most of all,
I am loving you
with all of my heart.

— Deanna Beisser

I Will Be There for You
Whenever You Need Me

Whenever you're feeling happy or sad,
   excited or confused,
and for some reason there doesn't seem
   to be anyone
with whom you can share those feelings,
I just want to assure you
that I'm here for you at those times,
beside you every step of the way.
You may need to be alone for a while;
I'll understand, and I'll stand back,
allowing you to think for yourself,
hoping that you're aware
   of my willingness to help you.
Let me know whenever you're
   in need of me,
and I'll be there for you,
because I love you.

— Chris Ardis

I'm on Your Side,
and I Always Will Be

I just want to give you
a few words of encouragement . . .
to tell you that I believe you are
one of the best people around,
and someone who, without a doubt,
deserves to be happy
in your pursuits
and successful in your efforts.

I know that things don't always
    go as planned,
    and plans don't always
        work out as soon as they should.
But — because you are
    the great person that you are —
    I know that your hopes will
    eventually come true for you.

In the meantime . . .
if you ever need any cheering up,
or any words of encouragement,
all you have to do is let me know
        what you need.

Because I'm on your side . . .
        and I always will be.

— Adrian Rogers

To My Child, I Love You

I feel so fortunate to have you for a child
I love your bright face
when we talk seriously about the world
I love your smile
when you laugh at the inconsistencies in the world
I love your eyes
when you are showing emotion
I love your mind
when you are discovering new ideas
and creating dreams to follow
Many people tell me that
they cannot talk to their children
that they cannot wait for them to leave home
I want you to know
that I enjoy you so much and
I look forward to any time we can spend together
Not only are you my adored child
but you are also my friend
I am so proud of you
my child and
I love you

— Susan Polis Schutz

You Are a Wonderful Teenager
I Will Always Love and Care About

It's hard sometimes, when people
are changing their lives, to
understand each other, or even
to talk. You are struggling right
now for independence and the
right to live your own way . . .
and I sometimes struggle for
the strength to let you do it.
I wish now and then for the days
when a kiss or a hug could make
your world bright again; but
your world is more difficult now,
and you want to make your own
way in it — which is as it should be.

I only want you to know
that when you get hurt, I will
hurt for you; and that deep
down, I always have confidence
in your ability to find your place
in your world. If you ever need a
caring heart, or someone to listen
to your deepest dreams or concerns,
I will be there for you;
and remember, above all else . . .
that I love and care for you.

— M. Joye

ACKNOWLEDGMENTS

We gratefully acknowledge the permission granted by the following authors to reprint their works.

Char Weisel for "You Always Have My Love and Support" and "I Know It's Difficult . . . ." Copyright © Char Weisel, 1989. All rights reserved. Reprinted by permission.

Valerie J. Higgins for "Always Know that I Am Here . . . ." Copyright © Valerie J. Higgins, 1989. All rights reserved. Reprinted by permission.

Deanna Beisser for "A Special Thought from Your Parent" and "For a Teenager I Love with All My Heart." Copyright © Deanna Beisser, 1989. All rights reserved. Reprinted by permission.

Bettie Meschler for "I Want to Share This Special Thought . . . ." Copyright © Bettie Meschler, 1989. All rights reserved. Reprinted by permission.

Donna Levine for "Growing Up Is Never Easy" and "Accept Yourself for Who You Are . . . ." Copyright © Donna Levine, 1989. All rights reserved. Reprinted by permission.

David L. Weatherford for "A Message for You About Learning and Growing Up." Copyright © David L. Weatherford, 1989. All rights reserved. Reprinted by permission.

Barbara Allene Robinson for "Being a teenager can be hard; that's why . . . ." Copyright © Barbara Allene Robinson, 1989. All rights reserved. Reprinted by permission.

Sherrie L. Householder for "I Will Always Encourage You in Your Dreams." Copyright © Sherrie L. Householder, 1989. All rights reserved. Reprinted by permission.

Sandra Sturtz Hauss for "My Wish for You." Copyright © Sandra Sturtz Hauss, 1989. All rights reserved. Reprinted by permission.

Ann Rudacille for "Even Parents Can Make Mistakes Sometimes, Too." Copyright © Ann Rudacille, 1989. All rights reserved. Reprinted by permission.

Paula R. Hrbacek for "As You Go Through Your Teenage Years . . . ." Copyright © Paula R. Hrbacek, 1989. All rights reserved. Reprinted by permission.

Pam Lail for "You Make Me Grateful to Be Your Parent." Copyright © Pam Lail, 1989. All rights reserved. Reprinted by permission.

A careful effort has been made to trace the ownership of poems used in this anthology in order to obtain permission to reprint copyrighted materials and to give proper credit to the copyright owners.

If any error or omission has occurred, it is completely inadvertent, and we would like to make corrections in future editions provided that written notification is made to the publisher: BLUE MOUNTAIN PRESS, INC., P.O. BOX 4549, Boulder, Colorado 80306.